GARIFUNA 4 CHILDREN

Coloring Book
Numbers 1 - 10

Created by Isidra Sabio

Coloring Book "Numbers"

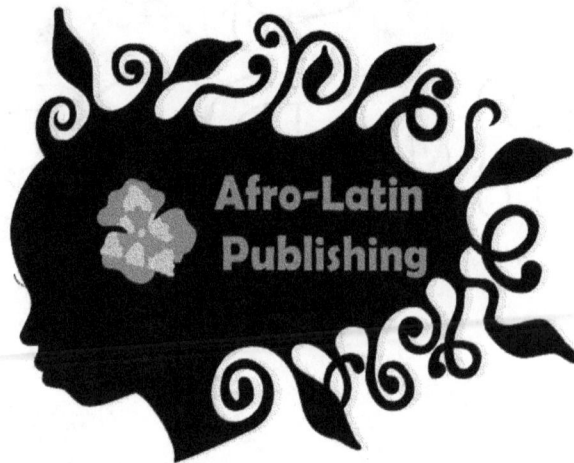

Afro-Latin
Publishing

ISBN: 978-0-9888240-0-3 (softcover)

Published by Afro-Latin Publishing, Inc.

Cover and illustrations by Isidra Sabio

Edited by Roy Cayetano

To order copies of this book

www.amazon.com

www.facebook.com/AfroLatinPublishing

Printed in USA

Introducción

The Garifuna language originated in the Island of St. Vincent prior to the Garifuna people's exile to Central America in 1797. The language is currently spoken by more than 100,000 Garifunas around the world, mainly, in Honduras, Guatemala, Belize, and in the United States.

On May 21st 2001, the UNESCO declared the Garifuna Language, Dance, and Music a **"Masterpiece of the Oral and Intangible Heritage of Humanity"**.

This coloring book was designed for children to have fun while learning the Garifuna language. This coloring book will help them learn how to count up to ten as well as name some elements of our daily life in Garifuna.

1

Aban Hewe

One Snake   Una Culebra

Two Stars

Dos Estrellas

Biama Waruguma

2

ürüwa Ganaru

Three Ducks

3

Tres Patos

Four Pigs

Cuatro Cerdos

4

Gádürü Buíruhu

5

Seingü Ban

Five Socks

Cinco Calcetines

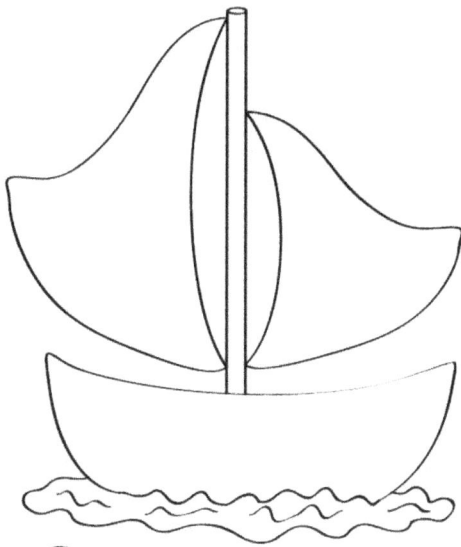

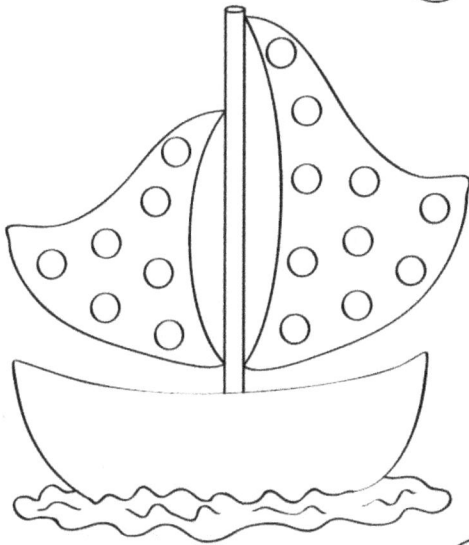

Seis Botes

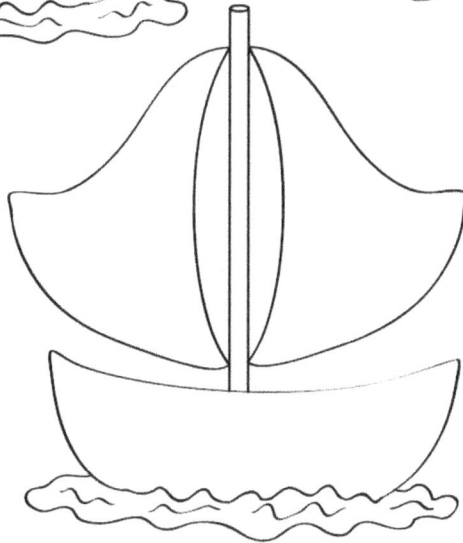

Six Boats

6

Sisi Guríera

Sedü Kopu

7

Seven Cups

Siete Tazas

Coffee

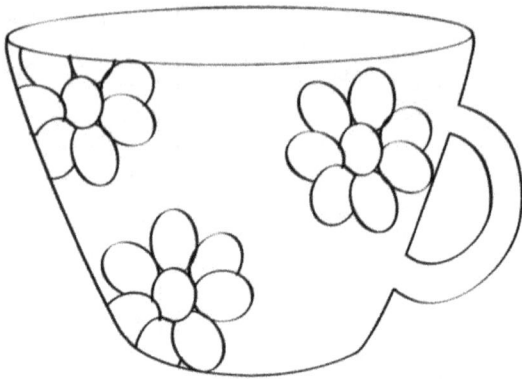

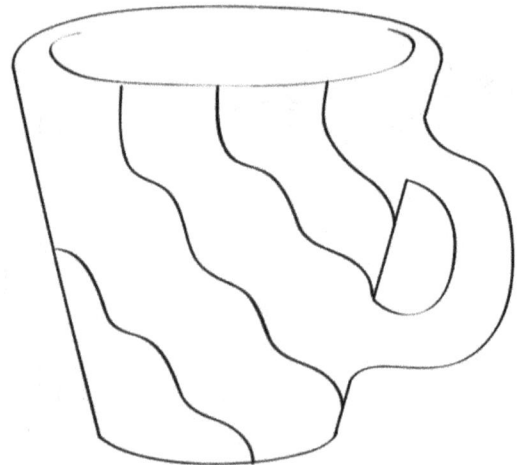

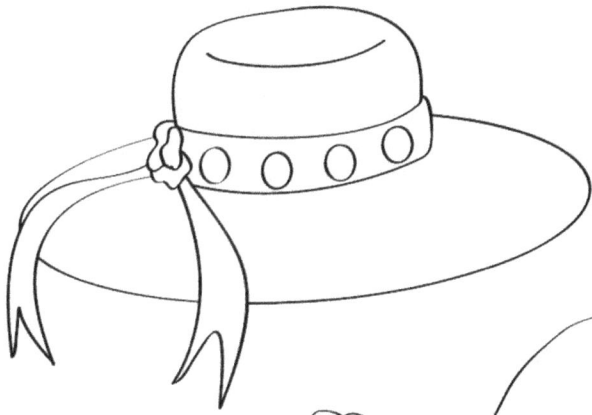

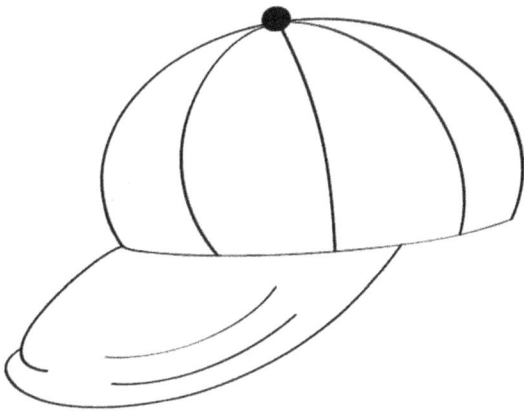

Widü Bunidi

Eight Hats

Ocho Sombreros

8

Nefu Sabadu

Nine Shoes

Nueve Zapatos

9

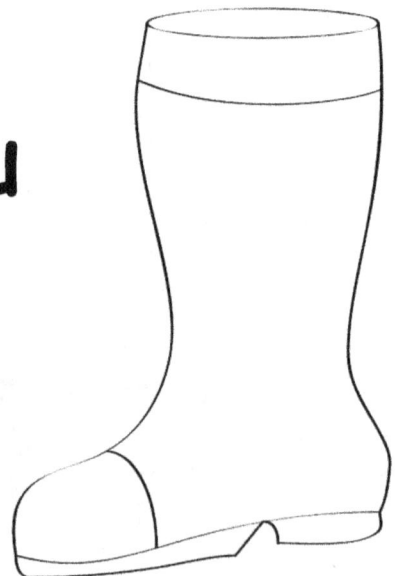

Ten Pumpkins

Diez Calabazas

Disi Wéiyama

Aban Ounli

1

One Dog

Un Perro

Two Butterflies

2

Biama Wurigabagaba

Dos Mariposas

ürüwa Garawoun

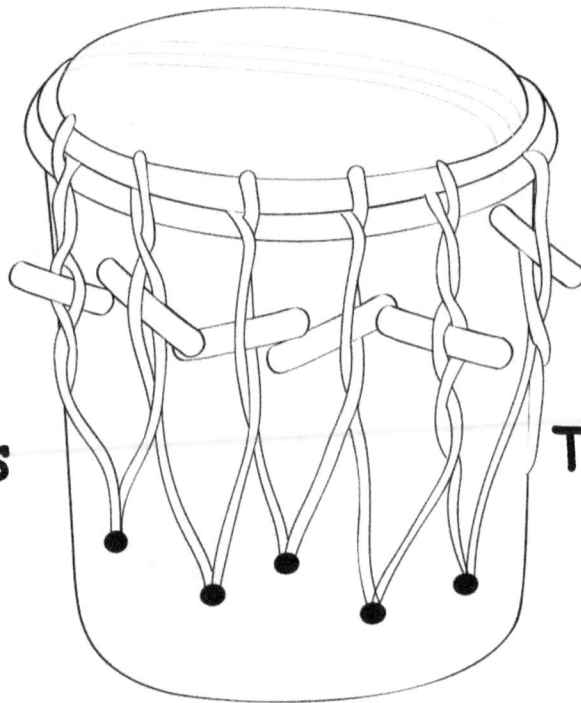

Three Drums

Tres Tambores

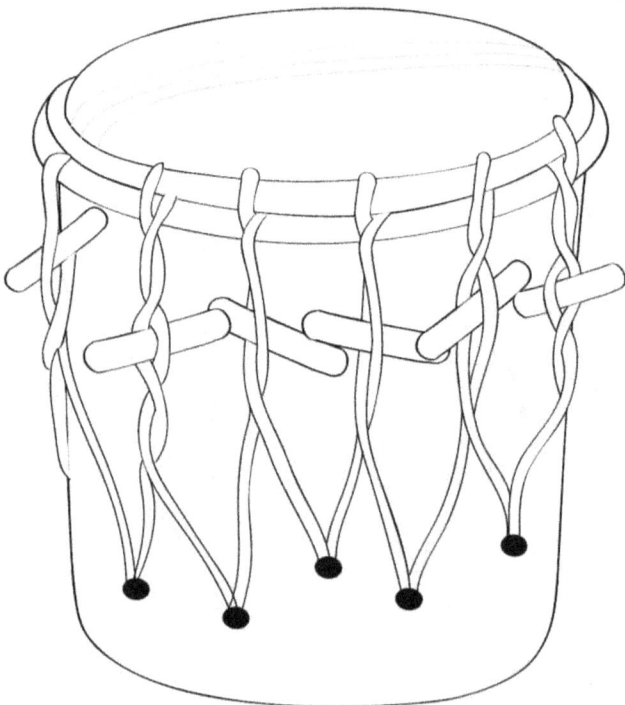

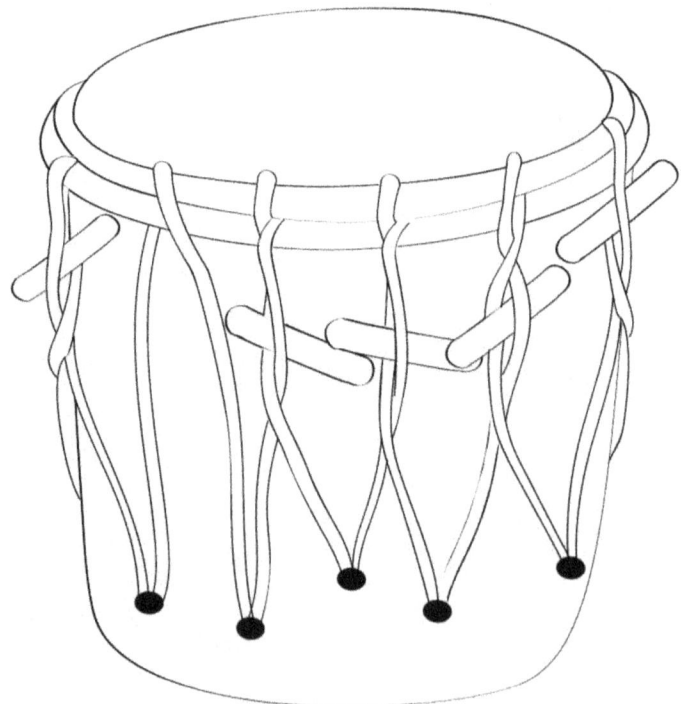

4

Gádürü Uduraü

Four Fish

Cuatro Peces

Seingü Húa

5

Five Frogs

Cinco Ranas

Six Trees

Seis Arboles

6

Sisi Idibu

Seven Beetles

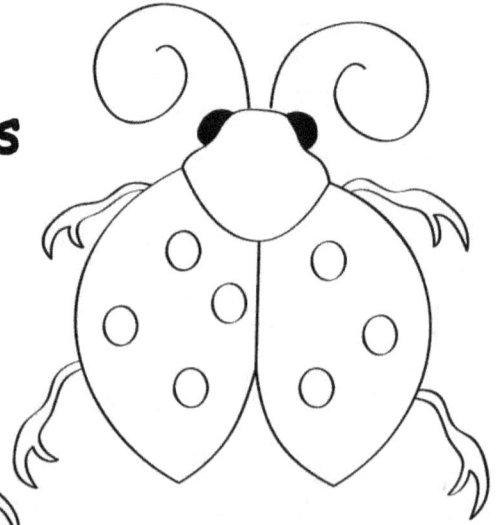

Siete Escarabajos

7 Sedü Deretágei

Eight Suns

Ocho Soles

8 Widü Weyu

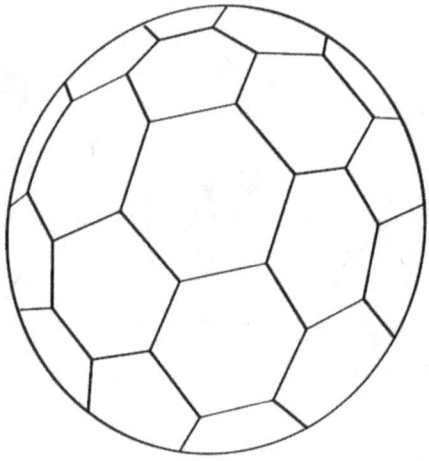

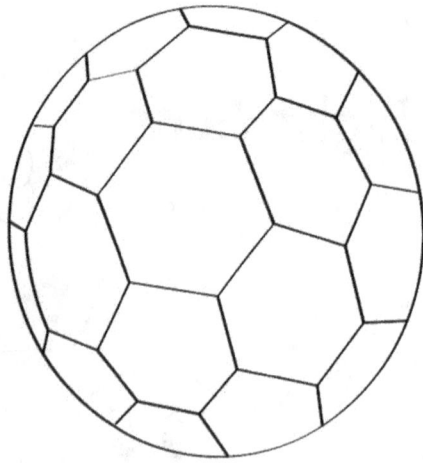

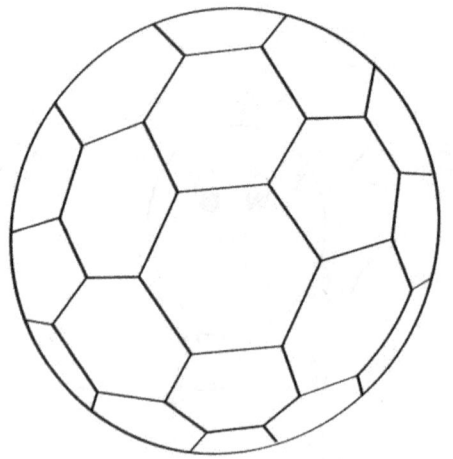

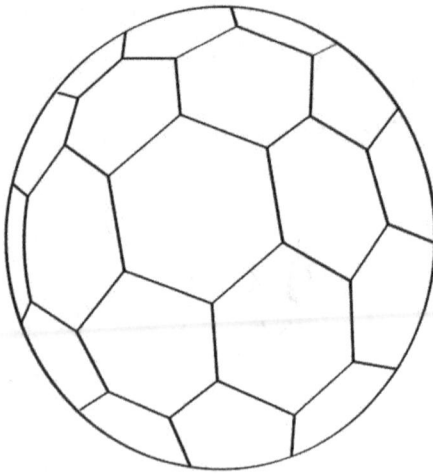

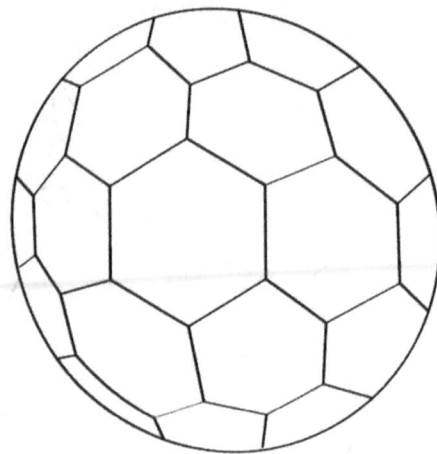

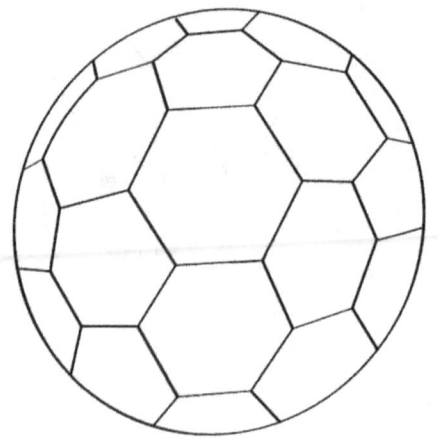

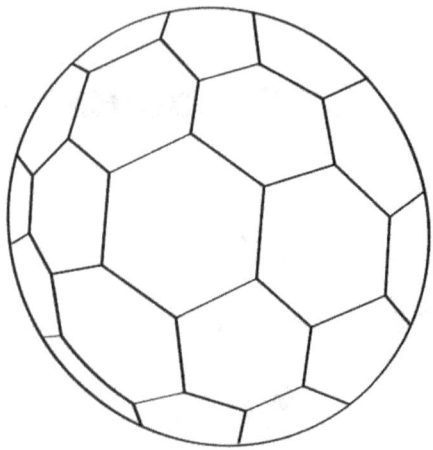

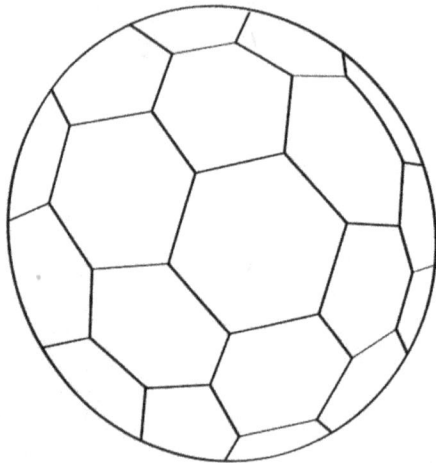

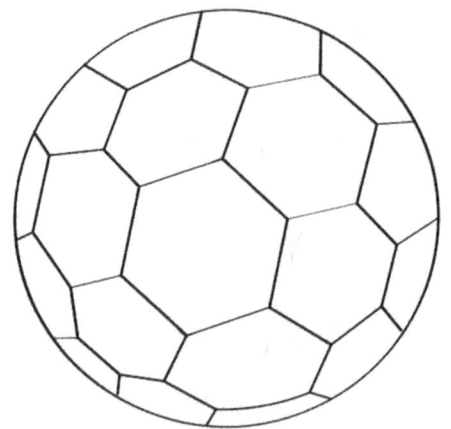

9

Nine Balls

Nueve Pelotas

Nefu Bali

10

Ten Bananas

Diez Bananas

Disi Bímina

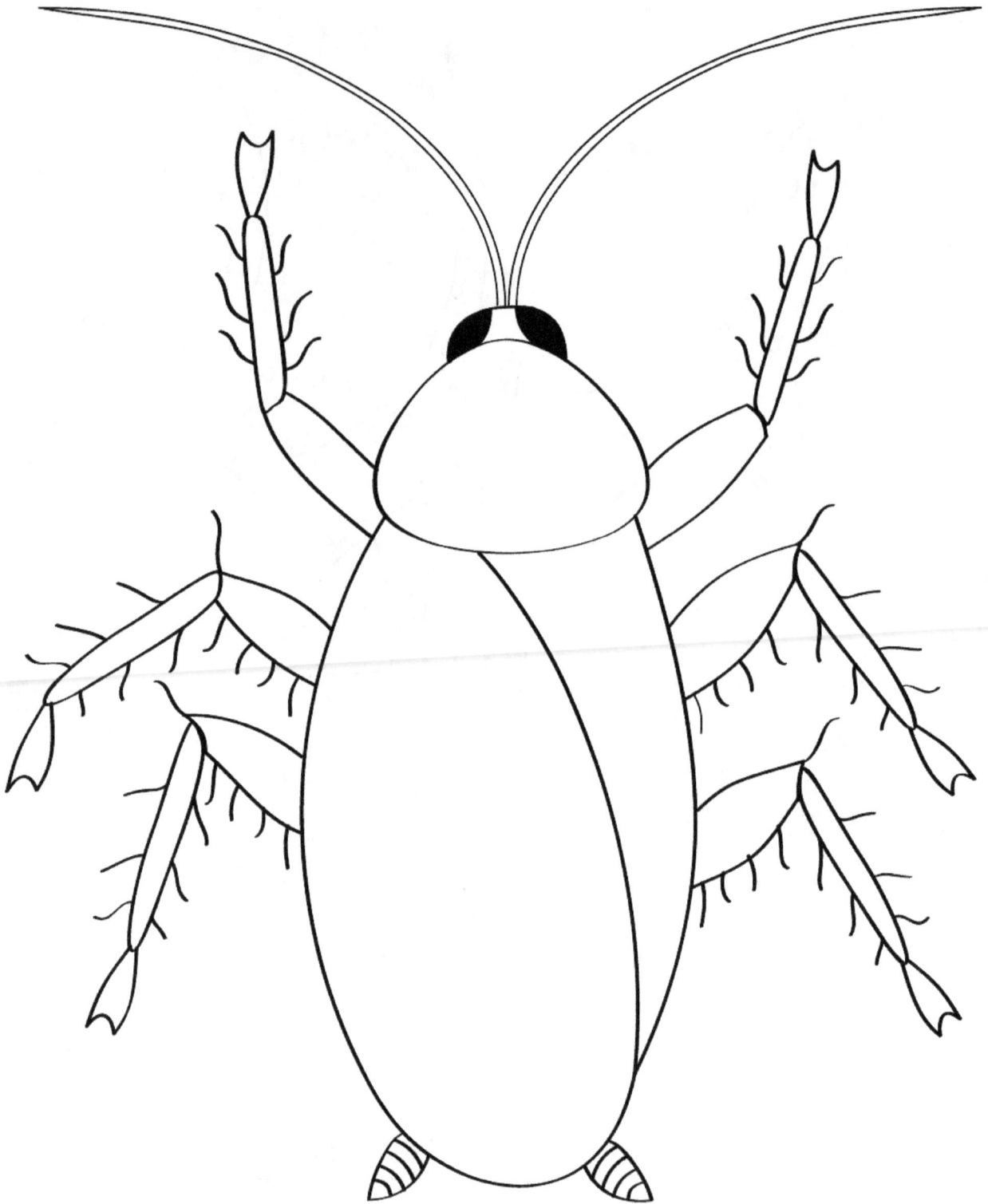

Cockroach   Cucaracha

Fudi

Garadun

Mouse   Ratón

Cow   Vaca

Bágasu

House   Casa

Muna

Guríera

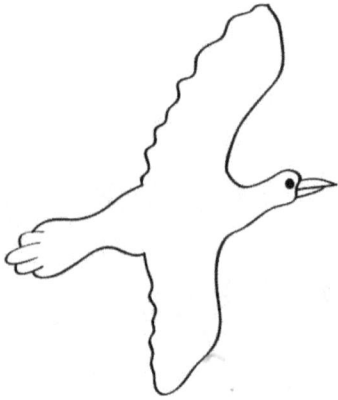

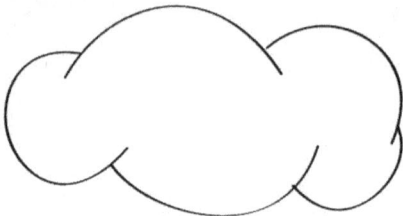
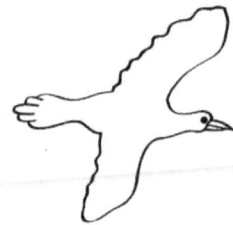

Boat

Bote

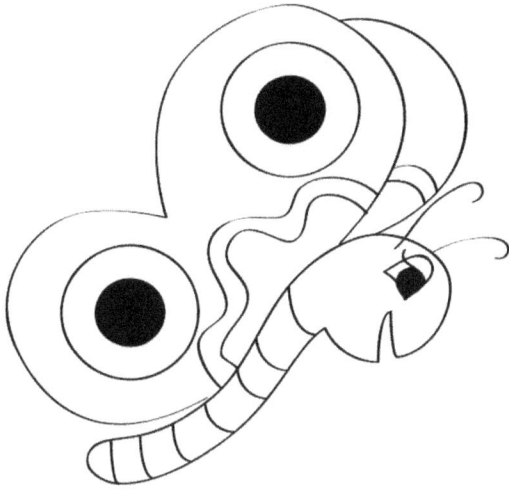

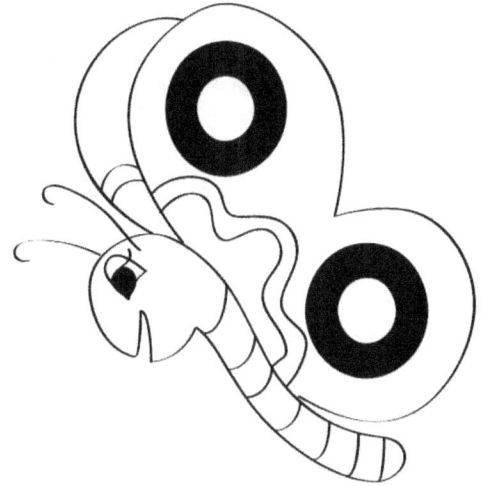

Fuluri

Flower

Flor

Beyabu

Beach

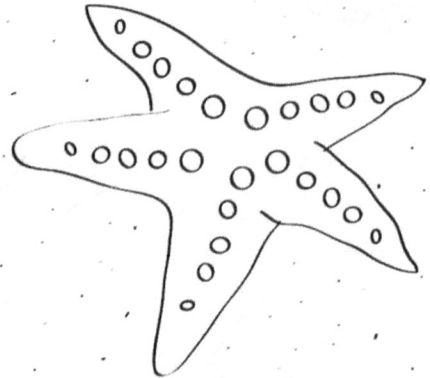

Playa

Isidra Sabio was born and raised in the Garifuna community of Cristales in Trujillo, Honduras. Isidra holds a Master of Science degree from Louisiana State University. In 2007, Isidra received a "Scientific Contribution" award presented by the President of Honduras. Currently, Isidra works as a Public Health researcher in the United States.

Isidra began drawing and illustrating when she was a little girl, she has several books in print for children and has created a line of greeting cards through her publishing company Afro-Latin Publishing, Inc.

www.ingramcontent.com/pod-product-compliance
Lightning Source LLC
Chambersburg PA
CBHW080536030426
42337CB00023B/4756